PLUMS & ASHES

Also available in the series:

*Eve Names the Animals* by Susan Donnelly
*Rain* by William Carpenter
*This Body of Silk* by Sue Ellen Thompson
*Valentino's Hair* by Yvonne Sapia
*The Holyoke* by Frank Gaspar
*Dangerous Life* by Lucia Maria Perillo
*Bright Moves* by J. Allyn Rosser
*The House Sails Out of Sight of Home* by George Mills
*In the Blood* by Carl Phillips
*The Eighth Continent* by Don Boes

*The Morse Poetry Prize*
Edited by Guy Rotella

DAVID MOOLTEN

# Plums & Ashes

THE 1994 MORSE
POETRY PRIZE
SELECTED AND
INTRODUCED BY
DAVID FERRY

Northeastern University Press
BOSTON

Northeastern University Press

Copyright 1994 by David Moolten

All rights reserved. Except for the quotation of short passages for the purposes of criticism and review, no part of this book may be reproduced in any form or by any means, electronic or mechanical, including photocopying, recording, or any information storage and retrieval system now known or to be invented, without written permission of the publisher.

*Library of Congress Cataloging-in-Publication Data*

Moolten, David, 1961–
   Plums & ashes / selected and introduced by David Ferry.
     p.  cm.  (The Morse Poetry Prize : 1994)
   ISBN 1-55553-208-X
   I. Ferry, David.  II. Title.  III. Title: Plums and ashes.  IV. Series
PS3563.O5539P58   1994
811'.54—dc          94-29229

Designed by Ann Twombly

Composed in Weiss by Graphic Composition, Inc., Athens, Georgia. Printed and bound by Thomson-Shore, Inc., Dexter, Michigan. The paper is Glatfelter Supple Opaque, an acid-free stock.

MANUFACTURED IN THE UNITED STATES OF AMERICA
98  97  96  95  94     5  4  3  2  1

*for my mother & father*

## ACKNOWLEDGMENTS

Grateful acknowledgment is made to the editors of the following publications in which these poems first appeared:

| | |
|---|---|
| *Boulevard* | Chemistry Set; The Enlightenment; Photograph. |
| *Georgia Review* | The Night. |
| *Indiana Review* | Having Come This Way. |
| *Kansas Quarterly* | Fireman's Carry. |
| *Kenyon Review* | 'Cuda. |
| *Poetry East* | Moths. |
| *Poetry Northwest* | Pinocchio. |
| *River Styx* | Housatonic; Voyeur. |
| *Sewanee Review* | Salem, Massachusetts; Camille Claudel and Auguste Rodin. |
| *Shenandoah* | At the Marine Corps War Memorial; Balance of Power; Flying; Brandy Station, Virginia; Losing It; Precision Bomb Run, Tokyo, 1945. |
| *Southern Poetry Review* | Freight; 1968. |
| *Southern Review* | Omission; The Brother I Never Had; Bio 7. |
| *Tar River Poetry* | Motorcycle Ward. |
| *Three Rivers Poetry Journal* | Inevitable. |

"Decisions" and "Magnavox" are reprinted from *Prairie Schooner* by permission of the University of Nebraska Press. Copyright 1994 by the University of Nebraska Press.

My thanks to the Pennsylvania Council on the Arts, whose literary fellowship helped me in the completion of this book.

# Contents

## I. MOTORCYCLE WARD

Inevitable  3
Chemistry Set  5
Bio 7  7
Freight  9
Housatonic  11
Motorcycle Ward  13
'Cuda  15
Decisions  18
Losing It  20
The Brother I Never Had  22

## II. THE ENLIGHTENMENT

Salem, Massachusetts  27
Moths  29
The Enlightenment  31
Voyeur  33
Flying  35

## III. BALANCE OF POWER

Pinocchio  39
1968  41

At the Marine Corps War Memorial   43
Precision Bomb Run, Tokyo, 1945   45
Brandy Station, Virginia   47
Balance of Power   48


IV. MAGNAVOX

Photograph   53
Camille Claudel and Auguste Rodin   55
The Night   56
Omission   58
Magnavox   60
Fireman's Carry   62
Having Come This Way   64

# Introduction

Take these lines as evidence of what is so admirable in Dr. Moolten's book. They are from a poem about Salem, Massachusetts, which is also a poem about American history, and about history, and about the condition we are in as human beings, tormenting one another in the name of justice:

> The whole dying town
> Seems to huddle against the immediate sea
> Of another winter. The black arts
> Everyone honed to a livelihood have been expunged
> By hard times: a foundry stands
> Cold kilned and rusting. The half-staffed
> Textile mills will never again spool
> The poor rough silk of the spirit.
> There is harsh reality in the air
> That frosts the windscreens of old cars
> Curbed along the narrow ways; who needs
> The ache of history? When I lean to touch
> The well-preserved foundation of Hawthorne's house,
> I know that the facts of this town,
> Like any facts, are old and mum as stone.

There is the austerity of the diction and the plainness and straightforwardness of the syntax that allow, among other things, figures of speech, when they occur, to count with maximum effect ("Textile mills will never again spool/The poor rough silk of the spirit"), not only because they are well and sparingly chosen and well expressed but because they are built from the same dispassionately observed factual material that they are interpretations of. "Who needs the ache of history?" The ache is the actual cold winter air of the seaside town;

metaphorically it is the pain of our history of injustice and poverty. The narrow ways are the actual narrow streets, and they are the curbing narrow ways of the terrible old days of injustice and the present days of poverty and decline. The cold air of winter frosts the windshields of the old cars; it is the reality of all these things, the history and condition of the town, that does so. This writing is close to the bone. And because it is so faithful to experience it knows the limitations of interpretation. Thus the sentence "I know that the facts of this town,/Like any facts, are old and mum as stone," with its wonderful word "mum," homely, and as mysterious as witchcraft.

Or these lines, from a poem called "Brandy Station, Virginia," near where a Civil War battle took place:

> They know
> That right there on the Fredericksburg-
> Winchester Road, survivors pulled pews
> Out of the St. James Episcopal Church,
> That having no time and "meaning no sacrilege"
> The men carpentered crudely, houses
> For the dead from the house of God.
> They can describe, with painstaking precision,
> The rifle pits, the rations and harnesses,
> The grade of bullets, the fire of logs
> And fence rails like a vigil light.
> Even I can reconstruct the encircling
> Dark wood, and crickets in the keen
> Of life, how the hearts of the living
> Eulogize with shrill fear and gratitude,
> With perseveration: *not me, not me, not me.*
> It was a week before the second Bull Run.

Again, the writing is plain as can be. The surprise of it, out of that plain narrative procedure, as painstaking as what it's describing, is in the wit of "the keen of life," and that keening of the insect would-be survivor is like that of the human survivors making the coffins, their mourning a compound of grief and of "shrill fear and gratitude" at having survived, persevered, so far. The poet's interpretive terms are derived as faithfully as possible from the materials they interpret: "Even I can reconstruct," so says the poem, respecting its own limitations, the perseveration of the insect life and the human life together singing, *"not me, not me,"* the creaturely survival song.

One trusts this writing because, though far from being unmoved by what it sees, it is dispassionate and steady in its gaze, always true to the materials it interprets. This is as much so of the poems in which the speaker is studying himself, his childhood, his manhood, his behavior, his own emotions, as it is of the poems studying our history. Take this passage from "Freight," a poem about a Christmas present of a toy train, given by parents whose marriage is troubled to a child already aware that this is so:

> It's the silence of my father,
> Studying me as I pull out the Lionel
> Strangled with tinsel, restraining his joy
> As I restrain mine. It's the silence
> Of his still hands, or my mother's eyes
> Brimming with pure water
> Before and after whatever happens,
> The dark looming power of his back as he turns
> And I wonder again where he's taking us.
> There's a small place in memory
> Where the route is a simple oval or figure-eight
> Where I fit the locomotive's flanges
> Back on the rails after I've run it too fast.
> But now I sense the true pull of iron
> Creaking under weight, the jolt of bad track
> On the crab claws which bind rolling stock.
>                               . . . now
> That massive train Dopplers past, rattling
> Its bones into silence, its stumbling family
> Of cars, shivering its one dim light.

The experience of the child, as he opens the charming present, prepares for the poem that will be made out of the materials of that experience, and the toy train in the poem suddenly looms large, frighteningly so, as that train of consequences which is the future history of the family.

Over and over again these poems demonstrate this kind of integrity. This is a true book by a true writer.

DAVID FERRY

*Er ist einer der bleibenden Boten,*
*der noch weit in die Turen der Toten*
*Schalen mit rühmlichen Fruchten hält.*

—Rainer Maria Rilke

PART I

*Motorcycle Ward*

## Inevitable

It is inevitable,
The trip to Dairy Queen
After they've fought
Again, Route 30, which is
Commonwealth Avenue
Only near the city,
Past Lake Cochituate,
The moored boats sudden
And epiphanous against low trees,
Like ducks capable
Of strange proportions
In the dark. My mother is clasped
In the back seat
Among us like a doll,
So breakable, and always fog
Ruins the highway bridge,
At least in the lie
Of memory, turning
Into the beams like someone
Surprised, a hand held out,
The fog rolling in
In great clouds of confusion
And blindness. I imagine the life
In the button eyes of ducks
As they glide stupidly towards me
On this same lake in daylight
Naive as children
Just from the throwing motion
Of my empty hand. I watch the shape
Of my father against
The windshield, the streetlamps
Bursting like flowers
Against the glass,

And my sisters touch me
And I don't mind. We sit,
Quiet as adults, hoping
That whoever is driving
Out in front might help us
Ferry our fragile cargo home
In this scudded boat
Of a Pontiac because he knows
Where to go and signals us
Deliberately keeping
An even, careful speed,
Letting us follow
His taillights out of there.

## Chemistry Set

In the basement, by the bright eye
Of the strung, bare light bulb, I'm
Seven years old, and I'm making things,
Scraping tannic acid, sodium bismuth
Into plastic flasks, or a little
Baking soda I mix with vinegar
To "see what happens" again and again,
Dumb luck when nothing bursts into flame.
The periodic table hangs like a strange
Alphabet on the wall, I read textbooks
About elements and atoms, everything
I discover makes sense and fits together.
I'm lost in my own little world
As my mother likes to say, and she
Has to yell, "Are you burning things?"
From the top of the stairs, the way mothers
Always detect the undetectable odors
Of childhood. Through the small window
I hear our half-breed Labrador, who will
Soon disappear in the earth, followed
By grandparents, the older uncles,
A chain reaction that begins as slow
As rust. I hear the mower quit,
Watch my father wipe his sweat and walk
From view as he'll do for good in just
Four years after one explosive crisis
Too many—the family better apart,
Less combustible, like the women
Who will burn me later or whom I will burn.
But I'm just seven, a neophyte
At abstractions like love. "No," I yell
To my mother. I have not yet discovered
Fire, which for me comes at the end

Of the age of reason. I still have
What she lovingly terms natural
Curiosity—my face stifled against
Flasks which do nothing but seltzer,
Like each day in the little world
Repeating the same blind experiment,
Hardly science—unaware that knowledge
Itself is mostly trial, mostly error.

## Bio 7

The year of their ultimate squalor,
Of my father's gum-chewing brunette
With the legs and the split quartz grey eyes,
Of my mother's overall violence, her premature
And less than sentimental eulogies for him,
Was the year of their separation.
It was also the year of the bad grades,
Of Bio 7, pithing frogs, and shucking
The durable exoskeleton of crayfish.
It was the year of Mr. Gordon,
Who pioneered us through each prosection
And made clear the vital and multitiered truths
Beneath all the slaughter. Many days
He kept me after, preaching mitosis
From the ancient slides, forcing me
To stare cross-eyed into microscopes
Until it made sense, telling me I hadn't
Fooled him, that he knew what was going on,
That I was bright, and that I could cry
If I had to. I remember how excited he became
Over prophase, when the invisible
DNA one assumed on faith, like heaven
Or honesty, thickened to jelly,
And metaphase, where under oil immersion
I actually saw the chromosomes paired
And lined up like intimate dancers
Or just plain lovers. And having seen
Endless acres of local prime cattle,
All that roan poundage back-crossed
To perfection, I conceived easily
Of the double helix and Mendel's peas.
Even with my blank stare and C–,
That we were just versions of our parents

Scrambled like cryptograms, seemed straightforward—
No rustic doctrine that genetics
Is the only code we're guaranteed to live by.
Perhaps beyond the empirical dice-throws,
The inexorable certainty of the whole affair
Clicked for me too, a process more stuck-switch
Than blind urge, the cells all machine-like
Precision, dividing and pressing on without
Passion or need. I remember the night
My parents explained, how I stared at them—
Him with my eyes, her with my jet-black hair—
Still trying to comprehend the point
They'd made, even as the cutting had begun.

# Freight

It's the spur track fallen into disuse
Which frightens with sudden life,
A forgotten bump in the road
Close to home, a brief Christmas display
Of bells and lights. But there's a lull
Before the boxcars thunder and pass
With their great burdens, before they rend
Their tunnel of sound, their hole
In the wind which the wind rushes into.
It's the silence of my father,
Studying me as I pull out the Lionel
Strangled with tinsel, restraining his joy
As I restrain mine. It's the silence
Of his still hands, or my mother's eyes
Brimming with pure water
Before and after whatever happens,
The dark looming power of his back as he turns
And I wonder again where he's taking us.
There's a small place in memory
Where the route is a simple oval or figure-eight
Where I fit the locomotive's flanges
Back on the rails after I've run it too fast.
But now I sense the true pull of iron
Creaking under weight, the jolt of bad track
On the crab claws which bind rolling stock.
When my eyes follow the dark caboose
I could be turning to look at our house
One last time the night I ran away. The pitch
Of a headlamp through the trees
Could be my father searching for me
With his flashlight, ready with his cargo
Of brooding explanations. My mother trails him,
Her face sad and open, and without

Their realizing I slip from a wall
Behind them, and follow in wordless acceptance,
Out onto the streets and years that come to this.
Life then was small, smaller than life, because
For children nothing is real, but now
That massive train Dopplers past, rattling
Its bones into silence, its stumbling family
Of cars, shivering its one dim light.

## Housatonic

This particular memory defies
The history that followed it simply
By carrying on in its own good time
Where dry road clay still blows
Through the headlamps of my father's bounding Jeep
On the way to night-fish in the Housatonic.
I believe a boy might just imagine
If he's young and naive enough
That all that bright dust has blown
Up into the mist of stars
He sees later on the jetty creaking
The drowned woodwinds of its pilings,
The way he might believe a prayer
Frail as a feather lure in his fluty voice
Which begins "Our Father who art in heaven,"
Refers to a man who smokes Winstons
And Vaselines his hair. It's been so long
I can't say for sure. I will say
That I loved the ignition of things,
Chasing lightning bugs with an old relish jar
Down by the water while my father
Kissed his hands into moments of brilliance
Putting a match to each chain-smoked cigarette.
Well, the fireflies died black and dry
As cloves, and I struck out across the years
Of his women, his moods, and his general intolerance,
And what escapes a fire anyway
Is just smoke, a flight of ashes,
And what are ashes anyway but the dust
Everything spoken or written says we are
Like my father dying with each bad habit
Into a man. But just now he stands
Bright as his hands above that black river

When I think of him, so that's what I believe
As if caught in the right light
Some dust can burn forever.

## 🍂 *Motorcycle Ward*

I can't say much about Richie Savalo,
A boy scraped out from under an eighteen-wheeler,
Except that he owned a Harley 650
And at sixteen I thought I couldn't live
Without one. I can't say I knew him
Beyond a ride or two and the day I joined
The other seniors who paraded to say goodbye
On the trauma floor. A surgeon—
Who tried to convince us that we didn't need
All that verb from a stoplight,
All that mind-altering power and open air
Like skinnydipping or TV made wild
And electric without the glass—proclaimed it
The motorcycle ward. We saw everything:
The long halls, the nurses passing sadly,
Each room identical, patients already
Partly embalmed in their casts. When we looked
They squinted back as though in some chrome glare
Beneath the syllabic drips of I.V.s—
That is, if they could surface through the morphine.
We found Richie, who they never quite
Pieced together with pins and prayer.
The day made me as green as when I first
Tried cigarettes. After that there would be
No bike, just a long line of slow-witted cars.
I can't say other effects were lasting
Although I did have nightmares for a while,
Not precisely about Richie or motorcycles,
The darkness more visceral than cinematic,
Which was perhaps merely the closeness
To the dead that comes with fear,
A sleeping empathy. There was only
The hair-trigger escape, the hurtling

Upwards or away from whatever bore down
On me until I felt that torque
Which the moment of waking brings
And over the dark terrain of the bedclothes,
I had outrun everything but a strange
Realization of luck and a terrible narration
In the thrumming cylinders of my heart.

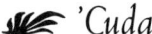 'Cuda

Yesterday, when you called me from where
They wring your body in rehabilitation,
And cried like static into the phone,
I wanted to say, this is not you anymore,

Forget your life as it is, let the receiver
Fall away as I do, summer, sandalled women
Along endless asphalt, black turf, glory again
Years ago, enough for both of us. Remember

How you used to swear there was nothing
Close, nothing that would ever shut you down,
Your '71 'Cuda, with its bored and blown
426 Hemi? Well, I believed you, racing

Alone all night in my bunk while our parents
Snored or tried to make another brother
Through the wafer-board walls. Rather
Than sleep I would listen for the chance

Screech and roar at an intersection
Rising somewhere from the gold sphere
Of mist that uptown became at night, sure
That it was you, and pretend I rode shotgun

Through that traffic of shadows, defending
Every stop light and woman on the boulevard
From the hated college boys whose lacquered
Foreign two-seaters were left finding

Second gear. Older, I cruised with you
And your girlfriends, smelled their beer
As perfume, watched you make them wet right there
On the leather seat; and I'm sorry now

I lied about my own nights, still a virgin
At sixteen when I followed you into
The mill. You said if there was any true
Likeness to the innards of an engine

In this world it was that place: metal dust
Searing as ash, arrow showers of sparks, booms
That swung and plunged while fires loomed
In vats; all day the roar ground us, a blast

Of steam down our throats, the world red-hot,
Water-cooled, sweat-oiled. I know we're both
Big, and you were bigger, with a bad mouth
And a good right, but when that plate hit

Your back, I knew you'd never walk again.
In the facility that you lived to loathe,
Where the spoon quivered each day to the mouth,
They claimed your hands might come back and then

Maybe your sex. Your wife wants children,
And you can't stand to think she'll bear
Only you, alive but miscarried somewhere
Inside yourself, the way that car you can

Never drive sits eaten by rain out back
With half a tank of gas, and lets the weeds
Embrace it with slow ruin. Go on, you said,
Take it, and finally I did, for your sake,

But I won't drive it. I still punch a clock
For the men born in white shirts and paisley
Ties, whose parted hair flutters in the AC
Of their offices. Their armpits used to reek

With real sweat under the exertion of facing me
While I helped all those adjusters and lawyers
Right the wrong, so you could lie for years
Totally snowed with Darvon. Sometimes I see

Their wives turn as I pass, to second the praise
Of my snug work clothes, the smell of Paris rising
From their breasts, because now that you're nothing
I'm the one they take raw and finish with their eyes.

All their laughing smiles remind me of a night
When I raced beside you, loving the whiff
Of high octane that seemed to never wear off
Your skin. We waited by the black iron gates

Of the University, the supercharger you bolted on,
Simmering, until an Austin-Healey nosed the line
At the light. The driver flicked his thumb down
While his blonde shook her head and laughed. On green

You let him have a length, and then all
At once, so smoothly, so evenly, your foot
Bore down the throttle like a man who puts
His root inside a woman because they will

Never have anything else, your Firestones
Scorching in every gear, your hand tossing
The shifter as the drivetrain whooped in passing,
The sidepipes emptying like twelve-gauge shotguns.

Shuddering with sheer torque, you sucked the chase
Right out of them. But pulling up at the light,
They were still laughing. They just sat
And loved it because they didn't care, because

They didn't give a goddamn what a true-
Run, boost-snorting, big block motor could do.

## Decisions

There we were, nearly men, with a fifth
Of Wild Turkey between us, on the roof
Of one Boston & Maine refrigerated boxcar
In a string of three sidelined on a rusty spur
Waist-deep in weeds. I had dared the others
And so would be the first to leap
From this one to the next, and standing
Amid the arrested explosion of stars
Had to decide in a quick dice roll of intuition
Could I do it, and was it worth it?
I hate to blame a woman when there were none,
Although we might have wished,
But I think I jumped in the name
Of a certain senior with frosted bangs, oblique
To me as the black rim of trees or my own experience,
Imagining somehow that the small ripple of the act
Against a breeze blowing in the wrong direction
Would change everything forever
And in a positive way. Certainly one whim
Or another drove me, because I did not know
How far away that other catwalk flew above the abyss
Of crushed stones, or how far my legs would take me,
And did not bother to even consider
This simple arithmetic. I just hurtled
And scrambled on the rutted steel
And congratulated faith. She would never
Reward my destiny, but I believe now
That a different kind of beauty rises
From such dilemmas even when one is not stupid
With love, and that out in the cold air that night
Some splendor in the moment beckoned me
With its door of opportunity that foresight
Promised to bang shut. I think every time

I resolve to walk down a deserted alley or veer
Into the oncoming lane to pass with heart and motor racing,
My decision comes to me as it did to Paris
Making his snap judgment that left a city
To burn for good beside the blade-glittered waves
Of the Mediterranean. It's as if a gambling ignorance
Were the same as mystery and could make
My fate profound: a terrible wrong goddess
I have chosen, and will choose again,
Wedded to the severe luck of who I am.

## ☙ Losing it

There's a coldness that makes a man a man;
   Call it the urge to take a mile;
Call it lonesome desire; I don't have it yet.
   I'm eighteen, thumbing home for Christmas,
Deep in the last year of my virginity,
   Deep in a blizzard on I-95 somewhere south
Of Pawtucket. All that frost layers me
   Into a snowman or something more perverse,
Something a woman's interrogating
   Headlights almost pass, but don't: pity
Or seasonal amnesty I take as pure epiphany
   Since women never stop. She's beautiful
And willing to take me all the way, headed down
   As she is, for Charleston. The heat
In her Ford half-broken, our breath fosters
   A fine mist, the gauges barely legible.
I've little sense for our condition.
   When she lets me spell her at the wheel
It's too cold outside, so she slides
   Across me, and the brief warmth of her jeans
In my lap brings me the chance of a lifetime.
   But for some reason I don't think
Of Joey Morocco asking, "How far did you get?"
   Or, "When are you gonna lose it?"
I don't feel whatever it is I'm supposed to feel.
   Tired, my grateful feet salvaged,
My hands considering no tricks, I just savor
   The road hiss, the strange affection
Of strangers between us. For hours each of us
   Consents to be weakened freight,
An odd symmetry, not equality, more a seesaw
   Kind of balance. But when I slam the door,
Turning to snow again as her taillights fade,

    I know I'm in for it, that the boys will razz me
For weeks. Well, late the same spring,
    I'll finally lose it. In fact, for years afterwards,
I'll keep losing it, a few women and more
    Than a few lives. Then one night, maybe tonight,
My wife asleep upstairs, pure mystery, I'll stare
    Through a lit window at my reflection
Standing in the snow, at what little I haven't lost
    Under the white powder of these years.
I'll breathe the same trust soft as a globe of fog
    On the glass, and remember the first woman
I ever loved, having gotten farther with the last,
    Like a car with bad heat still racing south,
A man good for the distance, or not a man at all.

## 🌿 The Brother I Never Had

I often forget you among the actual,
The women and ambitions that flit before me.
But that year I wished for you constantly,
Curled in my mind as in a science book
My father showed me once, like prawns
On ice in carts along the bay.
For six months you were all held breath
In our house while my parents contrived
And purchased and renovated. Cocksure
With trembling anticipation they even
Named you, the way I have often
Named the offspring of the great schemes
And romances of my life long before
The true labor of their incipience.
Impatient, I sometimes imagined that you
Had already arrived, following me
Around the house, a fantasy protégé,
Helping me collect insects like living jewels
Among the trees, chrysalides that turned
Brittle as ashes in jars. I felt
Guilty over each dead mantis or ladybug
But could never help myself. Possession
Is nine-tenths of love. We cage. We suffocate.
We cut open. Like the fragile larvae
Nothing moves of its own accord;
Like the county fair seedling, nothing grows
Fast enough. We can't wait to tear off
The pretty wrappers all in the name
Of the new and improved. My brother,
You were my first failure. You tried
To breech the world in May, too early.
Our mother screamed for both of you,
Whisked off in a bloody sling of sheets,

As from a car crash on the corner, the crowd
Oval with stares, summoned by the tattletale
Of sirens. I knew that my prayers
Had ruined things—what I now might call
Mind over matter, or more simply the will,
Violent with want. And if I was wrong
And guiltless, how many times have I been right?
How many women have I forced or rushed away?
How many undertakings have I hipshot
To pieces or smothered with obsession?
And if I was wrong, then at least
I had blame, which was better than nothing.
In the hushed waiting room, sad music played,
Sad then, sadder now. They wheeled her away—
Your waiting room different:
In the wrong place at the wrong time.
The whole uterus had to come out with you
Still inside, unfinished mystery like the slain
Goldless goose, the dry cocoons my prurient
Fingers once shelled open to find
Nothing but the dust of butterflies.

# PART II

# *The Enlightenment*

## ◢ Salem, Massachusetts

Here, the past is a rancid aftertaste
Like the tang of leaves in the salt-wet grass
Slowly turned to peat. Clouds that could be
The smoke from snuffed candles bluster
Over the bay's pale maples. The whole dying town
Seems to huddle against the immediate sea
Of another winter. The black arts
Everyone honed to a livelihood have been expunged
By hard times: a foundry stands
Cold kilned and rusting. The half-staffed
Textile mills will never again spool
The poor rough silk of the spirit.
There is harsh reality in the air
That frosts the windscreens of old cars
Curbed along the narrow ways; who needs
The ache of history? When I lean to touch
The well-preserved foundation of Hawthorne's house,
I know that the facts of this town
Like any facts, are old and mum as stone.
There was always suffering, and what suffering causes;
What can one say with compassion
That still has justice? What words are not more cruel
Or tender fiction, the stories
One life inscribes on another? It seems easy
In the learned light of centuries
To spell out the obvious, to accuse
The accusers who claimed each girl, bright as maize
At the height of her powers, stood over them
At night thin as a veil and touched them
Inside their heads, to insist
That like anyone she woke in the dark
Between them all, only wishing she could.
But where the hangings occurred a hundred years

Before Hawthorne described a bitterness
More indelible than the providence
That caused it, how the rubric of just one letter
Could imperil the flesh, nothing
Has erased the chill in the presiding wind.

## Moths

Three couples sit with after-dinner brandies,
Late May, small, high moon, the back porch
Like a delta with its current of lamplight
Flowing into the rest of the world's black sea.
The breeze makes everything flutter,
Even the moths which are nothing
But animated snippets of cloth
That have leaped from this blazer, that dress.
It's really the light they hunger for,
Swirling away their brief intoxicated lives.
The men might be in their forties,
The women a little younger, from the fine
Hatching which makes clocks of their faces.
The scented flesh and smooth nap of each
Soft belly and thigh could have come
From an endless roll of carpet-thick
Turkish damask. As always, their eyes
Brim with sex, and whatever they discuss—
Arcane wars, politics, even the poor
Who flare up in the same city, another street—
Tinkles with an aside of laughter, all
Luxuriant bored desire, as if the explosions
Splashed unnoticed far out in that ocean
Of solitude. Above them the moon drifts
Complacently, like the bright bulb
The cartoonist draws for an idea, a common
Thought that burns and never goes out.
But they can't think it. Instead
They flirt with its incandescence, blindly
Illuminated, in the way that a disrobing
Glance, a hand on the small of a back
Feels the same as making love, at least
Good enough. What's life without mystery?

One might ask, and they go on into
The wee hours until the sound of someone's
Delicate sleep is like fraying fabric.

## The Enlightenment

On business in Florida's cooler half,
Near St. Augustine, they stay with her mother's
Brother, who she says has a hand for enterprise
Rivals might call a fist. An unplanned stopover.
Matt says to not stay would be foolish; hotels
Are costly. As she sulks in the garden
Matt sits with the family, their airy voices
Filtered through the trees, somehow celestial.
They talk of architecture, the nearby fortress,
How the conquering Spanish craved triumph
More than gold, gliding past archipelagoes
Into a hundred harbors along the coast.
She stumbles in heels to a wall which overlooks
The sea, the harsh consorting of surf and rocks,
The stiff tack of a chartered boat. She hates
How her uncle navigates slack conscience
Into good fortune. She hates his children,
Their power to know nothing. Twenty years
Before, his glorious marriage depleted,
He had her out for her seventeenth birthday,
Dinner, dancing, the unintended stop, a few
Snifters of schnapps, and then he had her. She tells
Herself it hurt no one. She was, after all,
Curious. He said there were things he could
Teach her. Touching the Moorish stone she thinks
Of Spain: tin-plated patriarchs, brutal, but
In a way majestic, deified with knowledge.
They sired progress and deflowered whole
Peoples. Meeting her uncle is corrosive
As salt. Gin takes her down gently, soft music,
Ice a tiny carillon in the glass. She wants
To compare herself to this flower bed,
All tender cultivation, and pretend

The lineage is intact, all the ghosts
Of her lovers primitive and innocent.
Looking far out, she imagines the anachronism,
Commandeers the beat-up schooner coming
Hard about, the bosomed sails willfully pitched
As any man-of-war, while above it gulls
Drift like puffs of cannon smoke. She pictures
The tiny man at the bridge, chin tilted, stance
Firm, distant and untouchable as a god.

# Voyeur

A man watches a woman disrobe in a window,
Which is not unusual, except each has walked
On this earth for almost eighty years
To arrive at such epiphany. Confusing grief
With desire, he believes in the absolute
Loneliness of the dark, in liberation
Snap by snap from the chrysalis
Of a dress, pretends that this is his dead wife
Fluttering long ago in the footlights of a dive
In New Orleans to bear up their struggling lives.
How that crowd of red and sweaty faces
Envied him, he thinks amid the roses.
As if peering from shadows into the undrawn shades
Of his own life, he catches a bright glimpse
Through the sheer surface of longing—
As close as we come to some modest human beauty,
The body as epitome of the soul.
Because guilt and fear intertwine,
He keeps his visions to himself until one night
After bourbon, when his son wants to know
If he still misses his wife, the man leads him
Among trees and stars to the precarious edge
Of his neighbor's world to watch her unveil
For her bath at ten, hoping to redeem
One passion or another. When the son, who prefers
Principles to fantasy, storms off,
The man starts to wonder if he ever loved his wife.
Maybe she was nothing all those years
But the dim flash of thighs or quiver of buttocks.
It's you I love, he says to the wedding portrait
In its gold-edged pane above the fireplace.
It's you I know, he says to Polaroids
Of her cocooned in a hospital bed for the next life.

Then one evening the woman sees him,
And lets curtains fall as on a small stage.
But because to walk naked before someone
Is to enter an intimate unknown, she too hears
Raucous music from her past, finds herself
Flushed and a little less alone;
And because the bleakest salvation
Still saves, she imagines herself loved,
Less profane, perhaps, but well consumed, the flesh
Impervious to all dishonors but one.

## Flying

    They wake floating in a roomful
Of blown curtains, perfect except
    The seraphs can't quite lift them off.
And he tells her, he's dreamed his death.
    The mass still weighs on him
Although the months of nausea have ended,
    The doctors have showed him clear X-rays,
And proclaimed him free, at least for now.
    Driving to work he recalls the view box
Shimmering—his lungs translucent
    As the fragile wings of something
Endstage and transient, like the shadflies
    Which shower his car in a swirled galaxy
Off the steaming woods. She's less sure
    How it will happen. It's a crash she fears,
A bridge abutment, a pincered semi.
    He drives too fast, exceeds all judgment
And fear of limits. As he swerves between lanes,
    She sits at home in her robe with a finger
Of Scotch and some concept of him drifting
    Preciously away, although she can't
Sixth-sense the danger—the clutch kicked out
    As the gauge sweeps its revs, the deep
Operatic moan of the valve train, the roll
    Of the body wrung hard against the laws
Of nature. But if there is a sixth sense—
    And there is—it's of time, and he has it,
Lets it heighten the others. He mistakes
    A morning rush hour through the park
For that freedom, still in essence unattained,
    Mind-altering as love—in a word—flight.
The wind comes and comes, pure lift past
    The oleanders and thin strapping oaks

Which tooth the curves. He loves the life
    Larger than life in billboards and how
Glare jewels a landscape, each day the same
    Blind transcendence, although sometimes
He worries over tickets stashed
    In the glove box, or her, tipsy and alone
In the dark of all this forecast grief.
    It's then that he considers how the banal
Follows passion, like the shadflies who lose
    Even their one day of spring,
Turned to drops of rain on a windshield:
    Nothing swift enough to rise
From the plane of its own nature.

PART III

*Balance of Power*

## Pinocchio

A father kisses his son good night
With stories, lies to him, one can be sure,
Tells him the lies his father told him,
That old whopper about the wooden boy perhaps,
The one a carpenter carves into life
By teaching the lessons of life, as if flesh
Were not an end to itself, but a reward
For what he calls truth, a subtle animus,
An allegiance beyond this fiddle
Of crickets in half-moonlight and the spruce's
Shining leaves. The son has hands nimble
With small talents, legs that stand their ground
Without strings, can hear the woodpecker
Of his own heart knock holes in the hollow trunk
Of the tall tale, but he still believes,
The way an older boy trusts the red oak butt
Of a rifle as it pounds at his chest,
The epic struggles his father sands and varnishes
Into principles and fierce loyalties.
In this way the proving sands of Iwo Jima
Become a minefield at LZ-X-ray; it's all the same
Transcendence. What's lost in the change
That telling brings are details: the explosions
Buried again like apocrypha, black as knots
Below the sweet grain of mists and sugar palms,
Or the village shops, where craftsmen fashion limbs
From soft tropic timber, sad Geppettos
Hard at work tacking boys together, arm by arm,
And leg by leg. And who would tuck in his son
To the strange moral-less fable of Richard Nixon,
Waving from the White House lawn, proud as MacArthur
Walking into the surf at Corregidor to save himself,
His nose never growing, no matter how many times

The bombs rained on Cambodia, where the lies
Of his patriarchy first flourished like a dense wood?
More caskets than spirits have been whittled
From such trees. Ah, poor Pinocchio,
Disney has colored you wrong. You were born
Into good flesh like any boy. Someone planed you
Stiff with attention, spruced you into lumber
To build upon, so they could saw off
What they needed, until there was nothing left
But your story, the one your father must tell proudly
While his pining hands wring and tremble
As if still working their limp puppet of hate and love.

 1968

It must have been small comfort,
Their parallel sadness, two widows
Walking in tandem, arched beneath
Their age and invisible burdens.
They had come from Palermo
And it seemed in clothes and words
That they had never left. I remember
Mostly summer in Massachusetts . . .
Penumbral collage of afternoon, slow sun
Rough in the dust, the old road
Behind their house ending finally
In swamp. Boys, we waded naked
Among bitterns and sandpipers—a melee
Of splashing—we were after the same
Jittery fish, the pond scum thick
As ejaculate. I was not that old.
The widows turned when passing,
And would not allow themselves
To see our bodies, their heads bowed,
The way one defers to the dead in grief.
Perhaps it was because already
We had budded from our neutrality,
Because we were men, even if
We were not yet men, and did not know,
As they did, that the property—
The white cottages, the blue and sun-hazed hills
Of Sicily, were divided
Among us, that soon, we would learn
To lead wild duck with a shotgun,
That soon far away at the front,
We would be needed. . . . I can still imagine
Past the slam of their door, wanting then
To laugh, at their shawls and frowning

Downward gaze, and now only
To have been able to say, Here
It is different. . . . Except, in the same daydream
My father listens to the nightly news,
My mother frets over the birthdays
I have left, and the word *draft* itself
Blows around our old house.
I want to say, It's okay, I never went.
But they're dead, and won't listen. Too late
We imagine ourselves as someone's loss.
All I can do is consider how one of them,
Long ago, might have sat up in bed,
Feeling the veil of sleep blow off,
And instead of the other, curved and sturdy
Like that hill of years, might have imagined
This body, damp and naive,
It's brief noise against her.

## At the Marine Corps War Memorial

> "FLAG HERO FOUND DEAD . . . his death had been caused by exposure . . . alcohol . . . the post war years were not kind. . . . He wandered from his reservation . . . and tried vainly to find a place for himself. . . ."
> —The *New York Times*, Jan. 25, 1955

Six figures, the heaved-up Stars and Stripes:
They have the harsh beauty of bronze
And at thirty feet, the height of legends.
I feel it too, vicarious triumph,
As if I deserved the inheritance,
*Terra firma*, these colonial foothills
Deep in frittered magnolia. The last
Of the six was a Pima Indian. His hands
Drift too far back and do not quite
Touch the flag. He gazes upwards, but not,
I think, at the same gods. I consider
The subtle exemptions of the Republic,
The quiet war that carries on
With history like the muffled hum
Of a power saw pruning in the cemetery,
The cherry tree branches that clutch
And fall. My thoughts shift between
Iwo Jima's black sand and ash, and his
Reservation, the few river twists
And spooned-out bluffs where they still
Weave fine baskets and drink Johnny
Walker Red, the white bones of the desert,
Where nights fall cold, the stars clear
And sovereign. I focus on the statue
He became, for a moment dispossessed,
Although this is Virginia, the Capitol's

Garden, the smithed-iron sun still warm,
Slung into the trees. Late afternoon holds
Its reverent stillness, and the shadows
Fall long, as of a national will
That once rose lean and heroic.

# 🍂 Precision Bomb Run, Tokyo, 1945

This pilot behind the Plexiglas
Of his rumbling B-29 sees in all directions.
When the bomb bays empty, he will grin
Like a child striking a match.
Below him: a woman. What separates them:
More than 30,000 feet. She smiles at river lilies
Fragile as origami. The sirens
Have not yet sung. If he had seen her,
They might have been lovers; certainly he would not
Have killed her as she ran along the water
In her long black hair. Is this image too precise?
What about a nation's aggression:
Manchuria, Pearl Harbor? What about fascism
And democracy? Good and evil? The hero
As incarnation of the will of the people?
The trouble is, too much goes on already
In the high thin air of the idealized or hypothetical.
But bear with this: if two nations at war
Are their masses arranged obversely—each of us
Facing each of them—imagine these two
As such a pairing. Imagine her fine hands
Instead of those of the man deaf in a headset
Guarding a radar screen and all it portends,
The small blips not unlike a sick heart
On a monitor. Then imagine the pilot's heart,
Strong as it is, how she might steal it
Like a firefly loosed from a jar. And knowing her
Imagine how he might wish to be let go,
His "Super Fortress" veering wrongly in the sun
To leave its payload with the sea.
In this way we might have married all of Asia.
But war is the bastard we keep siring
And that day in Tokyo the bombs whistled

From a warm wet wind. The thump and smoke
Of the *ack-ack* was as loud as his heart.
There are silent truths below the history:
Paper lilies on the water that become
A woman's hands, the blood in wisps, how she floats
To a little shore among the broken trees,
The scattered oars, the silt undisturbed once more.
Imagine he lifts her beads from near his muddy shoes,
Imagine he takes her in his arms instead of soaring
In that high context of faith and duty.
Surely the cross hairs might have gone fuzzy,
Surely he would have nursed her back gently
In her half-wrecked fuselage, which is the way
The enemy leaves one wracked body and enters another.
But his pulse is strong, his opinion quick
As reflex. If he's in love, it's not with a woman
Lost in perspective and distance. Sharp-eyed
Like all of us in the tiny bubble
Of his life, he sees only sky and sky and sky.

## Brandy Station, Virginia

A few miles from here, they've unearthed
A young Confederate soldier.
The historians already know which night
He died, how far his elite unit tramped
Along the Rappahannock River
Through a limbo of gunsmoke, the burnt straw
And brimstone of dueling artillery,
The claiming of both sides. They know
That right there on the Fredricksburg-
Winchester Road, survivors pulled pews
Out of the St. James Episcopal Church,
That having no time and "meaning no sacrilege"
The men carpentered crudely, houses
For the dead from the house of God.
They can describe, with painstaking precision,
The rifle pits, the rations and harnesses,
The grade of bullets, the fire of logs
And fence rails like a vigil light.
Even I can reconstruct the encircling
Dark wood, and crickets in the keen
Of life, how the hearts of the living
Eulogize with shrill fear and gratitude,
With perseveration: *not me, not me, not me.*
It was a week before the second Bull Run.
The old brick church itself would fall later,
As churches fall in such a forest
Like a tree that makes no sound, and in more
Than a century they'd marvel over his skeleton,
The buttons from his coat, his pipe;
And the wood, perhaps they'd wonder
If it was ever holy or just wood,
Like the tall planks Christ was laid on.

## Balance of Power

If you stopped for a moment on highway 50
About ten miles east of Kinsley,
You might say this is the grace and center
Of our nation. You might stand and watch
The combines sail like frigates into the soft wheat,
And think of real fleets on real seas,
How beside the formal definitions
This too is a balance of power.
Then, if you took the side road out to the main house
You'd see how, close up, the paint peels
Like slow kindling in the sun, how in back
Three gutted cars go on making rust,
A chemical nostalgia for rare summer rain.
Out here, the sea is a theory. There are
No borders, unless you stretch your definition
To include the sky. The clouds drift, unreal
Against blue air and distance, the prairie
Seasonal as politics, although the war
Never ends against one attrition or another.
If you talked to the son back from Germany
Stepping down from the John Deere
In the silo's giant shadow, he'd call himself
One of the last of the Cold War vets.
You would never ask him if it was worth it,
Even when his father laughs at the prime rate
And news of more corporate farms, and says,
Sometimes it seems we're not in Kansas anymore.
He hates this talk of selling, of surrender.
The horizon tilts from blue to orange—
And the sunset, you might compare that accessible
Warmth to the great momentary peace
Filling the world. His father tallies
Large numbers in a child's spiral notebook

While on the kitchen table a soft wedge
Of cheese and breadcrumbs lie invisible
In the sun's wide shaft like what filters down
From unimaginable wealth. His mother
Would ask you if the air smelled like storm,
And you would say you didn't know,
Because you didn't, but they would be deep
Again in their own concerns. And as you turn
To leave they would fall silent, while outside
In darkness, the winds would pick up,
The clouds would roll on, like the forces
Of a vast empire they'd been fighting for so long.

# PART IV

# *Magnavox*

## ❧ Photograph

It's from before me, black and white.
You don't think you look like this
Anymore. I tell you not to say
Another word. Let me guess.
You stand outside on a patio,
Somewhere suburban, nicely stultifying,
With sloped roofs—and still air
Because the elegant birch
Does not blur. I admit though
I don't know the basic facts . . .
Was there sun? Is that a pink tea rose
Or a crimson rambler?
The short sleeves suggest
Warmth; the other people mostly
Have turned their backs but you
Smile, surprised, heel-raised,
Catlike, and the man
In the tuxedo you've upstaged,
His cigarette coyly cocked, tilts
His head in laughter, both of you
Filled with some transient pleasure.
Perhaps spring. Perhaps a wedding.
By your face I bet five years ago,
The year I drove over the mountains
Deep into Mexico, the year
You pulled away from yet
Another husband. I know you wear
A white dress. Somehow
With you I believe that's okay.
I think we both measure innocence
By intention. I feel I know
Which day of June this happened,
Which moment, as if I should have

Framed this shot myself,
Instead of standing
Three thousand miles away
Outside a cool crumbling church
Haggling over trinkets with campesinos.
I remember the sun came down hard
On the afternoon, how all I wanted
Was a beer. I didn't know
How predestined I had become,
Aimed at you like the 35mm lens
Which found this. I remember
The graceful ruins outside
Of town, how easy it seemed
For beauty to end like that.
Maybe your husband owned the camera
And didn't know you were already
Looking past him. Maybe afterwards
You filled youself with wine
And splendor, and laughter,
Or left early, because you
Wondered what the day meant.
I don't know. I have no more pictures
To go on. A few days later
I turned onto the Pan American Highway
And began the long trip
That ended here, sitting on your bed
With this snapshot. I laugh
Because you look at me and pretend
To hold a camera, and because
I want you so much. At home
I have color pictures of my trip,
Some, like the ones of the ruins,
With no people in them. Even with all
That sky and sun, they seem
So sad, so momentary.

## Camille Claudel and Auguste Rodin

Making love to him in that studio
Among the half-human lumps of clay, the Paris breeze
Corrupt with plaster dust, the hellish heat
From metal poured in casts, she must have understood,
More than anyone, that only his hands
Were sacred, or knew perfection, or savored
Their own genius. The rest of him was common, at times
Obscene, confusing flesh with marble
When he smoothed passion into his young life-studies.
But admiring his interpretations of hands
She must have seen his own penetrate angst
Into revelation—those great bronze hands
Rising out of bronze like a drowning man's
From a black sea—as if more than dying
It was his own medium he could not escape.
She might have wished she understood
The human condition as well when she worked
With lifeless things, could undress a soul
From stone the way a peasant tears into bread.
He drove her crazy with his lust while sweating
For years over an abacus of figures
For Dante's infernal Gate. She never knew
What it was to be a genius or maybe she knew, maybe
In a different time she would have better survived
Her gifts, but certainly she knew what it was
To love one, how his less talented heart
Strove to keep pace when those hands found her
In their grasp and submerged her in the dark bronze
Of the dark. She must have known that they groped
In just this way through every cloud
Of inspiration, that he failed them each time
As he failed her, that given the chance to pull
His frail body into heaven, he would have chosen
To let go instead, after stealing all that he could.

## The Night

I'm staring at my wife
In her tight black skirt and auburn hair.
I'm watching myself take her home.
I'm watching myself years ago
In my summer-weight wool and Oxfords
Amble along Chestnut from 19th
Back to Broad. It's a lovely night,
The trees standing soft and filled
With light like paper lanterns.
Lives flare in the windows
Like the Little Match Girl's matches.
The two of them can't help
But glance between the curtains, as if
Shopping for a future, choosing a mirror
And brown flowered wallpaper,
Maybe a sofa bed, maybe even the names
Of children. I walk behind them
Trying to whisper in their ears.
They don't know where they're going,
But I do. They half drag, half stumble upon
Each other in embrace. I tell them
To listen closely to each misstep.
I tell them to look: one by one, the lamps
Are going out. But this is the night.
Desire is safe here. And so is forgetting,
Which is where the future begins.
I breathe the warm air and imagine
The love that's coming: her face so close
He can't see what it looks like, his words
So low she can't hear them, and then
The pounding and squeaking of the flesh.
Somehow, I fend off the happiness.
I watch them lean into each other

Like two hands shielding a small flame.
They think the chill is their own adrenalin.
They think this is the night,
The mystery and the passion.
But it's only darkness, and more darkness
As if the match has burnt down
To the fingers, and is shaken out,
As if someone has kicked dirt
On their embers. I wish they would turn
From those stairs, this unlit room,
That they might walk softly away
Before that blanket gets pulled
Over everything, over their poor
Innocent bodies, before it blinds
And hides them like earth.

## Omission

A man opens the chest with his wife's old letters.
He can't help it; like the ripe plums she left
   In the crisper, it's there and she isn't.
She has driven to stay with a dying friend,
   And for the first time in years he's alone,
The house dark and empty. She could be the one
   Dead, the chest feathery as an urn of ashes.
Bowl of plums, urn of ashes—which is it?
   He digs in, devouring her parents' litanies,
Endless postcards from acquaintances.
   At the bottom he finds an old diary with pages
Torn out and a long entry about her lovers
   That starts midsentence. From the dates, he knows
That she wrote it before he'd won her over.
   But as if anticipating just this scenario
She has let runes stand for all the names.
   After making inimitable love, X has told her
She is beautiful and, with his rasping voice,
   Has crooned to her like a wounded bird. For paragraph
After paragraph she can't decide whether to take X
   Or stay with Y, who falls asleep in the middle
Of things, but who will dedicate his livelihood
   To her; such bountiful magic in both of them,
She writes. He wonders what she did, and which
   He is, the red hot lover, or old reliable,
And as if his teeth had cracked on the seed
   Which is the essence of fruit, everything
Seems to blossom from this fact—who she wanted,
   What she preferred, until he doesn't know her,
And it is so long ago he can't remember,
   Can't see himself as someone else. His voice
Fires up tunefully, and he thinks of foolish chances
   He has taken, romantic lies he has told, but also

Of how tired he becomes at the worst moments.
    He feels an odd sense of disembodiment,
As if his whole life were open to question.
    Perhaps if he sings she'll hear him across town,
As something different, a bird or a breeze, like memory
    Across time. Perhaps if he works harder,
She won't complain about breaking her back
    For spare change. He yawns; both seem
Like too much trouble. He doesn't consider
    The possibility of a third man, Z, a latecomer,
Missing, or in another book, whose magic is all
    Botched tricks. A man who hates music, and puts
Her to sleep with his cemented notions,
    Who can't even taste the difference between plums
And ashes, who takes her love, edging all rivals
    With nothing more than years.

## Magnavox

A man dreams of his dead mother's house,
Dreams he has come to live there again, a grown man,
But with a boy's gadget-loving hands
Turning the knobs and dials
On the old black and white television
That stands massive on its throw rug
Centering her living room. He knows that soon
His mother will arrive and feel the screen
For warmth, the old picture tube screen
In its fake walnut case, and look for the star
In the center, the star that takes so long
To disappear after the set clicks off, that even now
Just sits there like Venus on the horizon or the polestar.
He knows that he is punished, that he has been forbidden
To watch, and that from these simple tests
His mother will learn that he has granted
His own amnesty, which is what he wants to do
Right now in his sleep, find an excuse,
A clever supplication, to pardon himself
From the snowy console of his own thoughts
On which the past plays itself over and over.
He flicks the set on and off and still sees nothing
But that star, its dark green field like a section
Of sky, a frame of warmth concentrating
His mother like light. Just this once, he dreams,
Let the evidence that brings grief
Disappear in time. If he could only imagine,
In the midst of a night like this, how many houses
Have darkened with people like him
Dreaming some human brilliance, until all the dead
Rise as unspoken thoughts, so small, so unassuming,
To form the constellations as we know them;
If only in this way true memory could enter our lives,

Focused at a safe distance. Then he wakes and discovers
It's a dream, and actually says this out loud.
But before long he sleeps again
And soon enough morning descends,
Filling the trees lined like one long eyelash
Above the valley, filling his ache
With the visible lines that have become his face
And the house once more with his own familiar things,
The sky full of fire so white, someone who believes
An entire life can pass in a single night
That never ends, might think
A star had smashed on the ridge.

## Fireman's Carry

A woman saved him, after the death,
After he sat for hours drinking alone.
She let him take her home. She liked
His sad, honest come-on line.
Perhaps she saw he was living
In the truth . . . no, better yet, lost in it.
And could be trusted.
Or perhaps it was the way death soaked him
Like wine a fricassee, rarified him,
Made him tender through and through.
Perhaps she was just being maternal
The way he could never be without
Wanting something else. Maybe
She wanted something else.
Except she held him as if supporting
His whole weight, and he remembered
The way his father taught his mother and sister
The fireman's carry, how anyone could bear
Anyone if they just distributed the effort
Over their whole body. And there he was:
Grief like a burning house.
Outside, the moon showed with a wedge
Taken, then blinked into mist,
Just as love, the human lie,
Saves more through its dousing of the light.
And on this last day of a life, this last
Clear day, he let it convey
Its black ladder under him, lying weightless
In her arms while the water
Of her hands steeped his whole body.
Without realizing, she found the day
Before and the day before that—
All the doors of his past.

Soon she would discover how they led
To rooms in the wrong house,
The one in which he lived,
That these flames were never his.

## Having Come This Way

What is memory if not a sense of direction?
Those geese on Cochituate's blue paper lake
Perfectly still as it began to flare
With sun laid directly against it
As if there were a fiery furnace
In which all living things live
With the perfect faith needed
And every moment of the past tested and retested
In that kind of crucible, and the geese
With their sudden fluttering sense of home
Not trying to evade it, but feeling their way
Towards its available fire,
Clumsily, noisily, like all our wishes and hopes
Wondering if they should take this breeze
And where, riding the laziness of the day
Up into great sheets of lucid air,
Then skimming the flaming water once more.
But the lightest hours travel farthest
And only when I look back now
Through the arches of rooms with no ceilings
That become the softly ruddying trees
Do the geese drift farther and farther
In their own warm light,
As if deciding at last
As if always flying south when I think of them.

A NOTE ON THE AUTHOR

David N. Moolten, born in Boston in 1961, received his A.B. from Harvard College in 1982 and his M.D. from the University of Pennsylvania School of Medicine in 1987. He currently resides in Philadelphia, where he is employed as a physician by the American Red Cross. His poems have appeared in *The Georgia Review, The Southern Review, The Kenyon Review,* and *Poetry,* among other magazines and periodicals. He has received a number of awards, including a Pennsylvania Council on the Arts Fellowship Grant in Literature.


A NOTE ON THE PRIZE

The Samuel French Morse Poetry Prize was established in 1983 by the Northeastern University Department of English in order to honor Professor Morse's distinguished career as teacher, scholar, and poet. The members of the prize committee are Francis C. Blessington, Joseph deRoche, Victor Howes, Ruth Lepson, Stuart Peterfreund, P. Carey Reid, and Guy Rotella.

### OHIO UNIVERSITY LIBRARY

Please return this book as soon as you have finished with it. In order to avoid a fine it must be returned by the latest date stamped below. All books are subject to recall after two weeks or immediately if needed for reserve.

JUN 16 1995

QUARTER LOAN

MAY 3 0 1995

JAN 0 5 1996